The Rourke Guide to State Symbols

HISTORIC SITES AND MONUMENTS

David and Patricia Armentrout

Rourke Publishing LLC
Vero Beach, Florida 32964

© 2002 Rourke Publishing LLC

www.rourkepublishing.com

PHOTO CREDITS:
©James P. Rowan pages 11, 12, 13, 16, 18, 19 top, 23, 28 bottom, 32 bottom, 34
©National Park Service pages 7, 15, 17, 20, 24, 27, 30, 35, 36, 37, 38, 40, 46, 47
©PhotoDisc pages 6, 8, 9, 10, 14, 21, 22, 25, 26, 31, 32 top, 39, 41, 42, 44, 45, 48
©Hulton/Getty pages 5, 28 top, 29
©Corbis Images page 19 bottom
©State of Vermont, Bennington Battle Monument page 43

COVER ILLUSTRATION: Jim Spence

EDITORIAL SERVICES:
Pamela Schroeder

Library of Congress Cataloging-in-Publication Data

Armentrout, David and Patricia
  Historic sites and monuments / David and Patricia Armentrout
    p. cm. — (The Rourke guide to state symbols)
  Includes index
  Summary: Describes a variety of historic sites and monuments, from the Alabama-Tuskegee Institute National Historic Site to the Wyoming-Devils Tower National Monument.
  ISBN 1-58952-085-8
   1. Historic sites—United States—Juvenile literature. 2. Monuments—United States—Juvenile literature. 3. United States—History, Local—Juvenile literature. [1. Historic sites. 2. Monuments. 3. United States—History.] I. Armentrout, Patricia, 1960- II. Title. III. Series.

E159 .A76 2001
973—dc21   2001031976

Printed in the USA

TABLE OF CONTENTS

INTRODUCTION

Historic places are important to all of us. They teach us about our past. They show us how far we have come as a civilization. They remind us how important it is to plan for the future.

As a nation, we take pride in our history. We set aside places that have special meaning to us. The places we choose are as different as the backgrounds we come from. From Native Americans to recent immigrants, we all have stories to tell.

The United States Department of the Interior decides which places will be chosen as national historic sites. Because the job is so big, the department created the National Park Service. Its job is to manage all national parks, historic sites, landmarks, memorials, and monuments. The National Park Service protects and cares for our national historic places.

Not all historic places are chosen to become national sites. Some historic places and monuments are important to only one part of the country. These areas are managed by the state or city where they are located. Some places or sites are managed by private organizations.

ALABAMA

Tuskegee Institute National Historic Site

Tuskegee University was founded for black students in 1881. Its first principal was Booker T. Washington. One of its most famous teachers was American scientist George Washington Carver. The historic site includes the George Washington Carver Museum and the Daniel James Memorial Hall. The hall has exhibits from the "Tuskegee Airmen," a group of black pilots who trained there during World War II.

ALASKA

Denali National Park

Alaska has some of the nation's most beautiful parks. One of the largest is Denali National Park in central Alaska. Denali, also known as Mt. McKinley, is the highest peak in North America and is located in the park. The mountain reaches 20,320 feet (6,194 m) above sea level. Wild

animals such as brown bear, wolves, and moose live in its shadow.

ARIZONA

Grand Canyon National Park

The Grand Canyon is one of the most beautiful places in the world. Nearly 4 million people visit the canyon each year. The canyon is more than 200 miles (322 km) long and almost a mile (1.6 km) deep in places. Visitors can see cliff dwellings

and other prehistoric ruins. John Wesley Powell and his group of men traveled the length of the canyon on the Colorado River in 1869. They were the first to travel the canyon by boat.

ARKANSAS

Arkansas Post National Memorial

The Arkansas Post was built in 1686 near the Quapaw Indian village. It began as a trading post for settlers and frontiersmen. Its location was important to the French, Spanish, and American armies during the American Revolution. However, its location on the Arkansas River was even more important during the Civil War. A Confederate fort was destroyed by Union forces there in 1863. Today the Arkansas Post is a peaceful place to visit. The memorial and a museum describe the Post's important history.

CALIFORNIA
Yosemite National Park

Named as a National Park in 1890, Yosemite continues to be one of the nation's favorite parks. Its most popular attractions include Yosemite Falls, Bridalveil Falls, and a granite mountain called El Capitan. The park also has large groves of giant sequoia trees.

Yosemite was a favorite place of John Muir. He proved that the Yosemite Valley was formed by glaciers. Muir is often called the "Father of our National Park System."

COLORADO
Mesa Verde National Park

The Mesa Verde cliff dwellings were discovered by cowboys more than 100 years ago. The Anasazi Indians built the stone buildings under overhanging cliffs. Not much is known about the Anasazi people. Researchers have learned that some of the ruins are nearly 1,400 years old. No one knows why, but the Anasazi deserted the cliff dwellings about 700 years ago. The people are gone, but the remains of their amazing and ancient city can still be seen.

CONNECTICUT
Replica of the Amistad

    Amistad was a Spanish ship used in the slave trade in the 1800s. A replica, or copy, was built in Mystic, Connecticut. The *Amistad* is famous for a court case tried by the U.S. Supreme Court in 1841. The *Amistad* carried illegal slaves from Africa to Cuba. The slaves fought for their freedom and took control of the ship. They forced the crew to sail back to Africa. However, the *Amistad* was stopped by a U.S. warship. The slaves were held as pirates and taken to the U.S. The slaves were tried and the Supreme Court ruled that the men were free.

DELAWARE

Fort Delaware State Park

Fort Delaware was built on Pea Patch Island in the Delaware River. The fort has five sides and covers 6 acres (2.4 ha). The granite walls are 32 feet (9.8 m) high and between 7 and 30 feet (3 and 9.1 m) thick. Surrounding the fort is a moat. To enter the fort people cross a drawbridge.

Fort Delaware once served as a prison for Confederate prisoners of war. More than 12,000 prisoners were held there at one time. Many of them were captured at the famous Battle of Gettysburg.

FLORIDA

Saint Augustine

Saint Augustine is the oldest city in the U.S. In 1513 Spanish explorer Ponce de León landed on the beach looking for the Fountain of Youth. He claimed the land for Spain. The French built a colony there in 1564, but the Spanish destroyed it. The city of Saint Augustine was founded in 1565. The oldest U.S. fort, Castillo de San Marcos, stands at the historic site.

GEORGIA

Fort Pulaski National Monument

Fort Pulaski was named after American Revolution hero General Casimir Pulaski. The fort sits on Cockspur Island near Savannah, Georgia. It is 32 feet (10 m) high. The walls range from 7-11 feet (2-3 m) thick and are surrounded by a moat. In 1862 the Confederate army defended the fort from Union army cannon fire. The battle lasted 29 hours. The fort was heavily damaged and was captured by Union soldiers.

HAWAII

Pu`uhonua o Honaunau
National Historic Park

Pu`uhonua o Honaunau can be hard to say. However, it is easy to see why its history is treasured by Native Hawaiians. The 182-acre (73.65-ha) park has temples, ponds, and ancient village sites.

In ancient times, if Hawaiians broke a law of the gods, they could come to this place to escape death. "Pu`uhonua" means refuge. A refuge is a place to go for protection. Once inside the refuge, a priest could forgive the sins of the lawbreaker.

IDAHO

Craters of the Moon National Monument

Craters of the Moon became a National Monument in 1924. In 2000 President Clinton made the park larger. It now covers 83 square miles (215 sq km). The area is a huge volcanic lava field. Scientists think 60 different lava flows cover the surface. The lava flows are 2,000 to 15,000 years old. Volcanic activity created the beautiful natural features. Park visitors hike or drive along trails that lead to many of the interesting sites.

ILLINOIS

Lincoln's Home National Historic Site

Located in Springfield, Illinois, this National Historic Site was the home of Abraham Lincoln. Mr. Lincoln and his wife Mary lived in this house from 1844 until 1861, when he was elected President. The National Park Service restored the home to its 1860 appearance. The surrounding neighborhood is also being restored so that the area looks much as it did when Lincoln lived there.

INDIANA

George Rogers Clark National Historic Park

In 1779 Lieutenant George Rogers Clark led an army of frontiersmen. He fought against British Lieutenant Governor Henry Hamilton and his soldiers. Clark and his men defeated the British army and captured Fort Sackville. The victory is considered one of the great battles of the American Revolution. A memorial stands on the site near Vincennes, Indiana. It honors Clark and his men.

IOWA

Herbert Hoover National Historic Site

Herbert Hoover was the 31st President of the United States. The Herbert Hoover National Historic Site honors his life. There, tourists visit the small cottage where President Hoover was born. Other buildings include a blacksmith shop, a school house, and a Quaker Church where Hoover's family worshiped. When you visit, be sure to stop in at the Herbert Hoover Presidential Library and Museum.

KANSAS

Fort Larned Historic Site

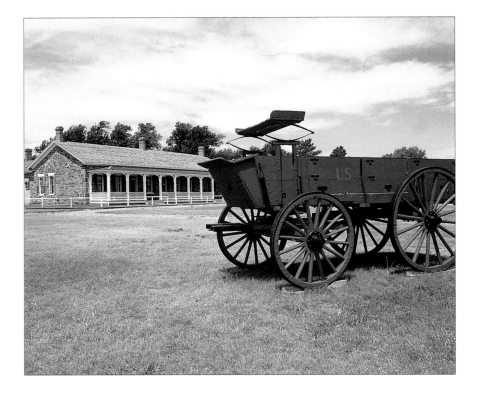

Fort Larned was built in 1859. Its purpose was to protect settlers who used the Santa Fe Trail. Hostile Native Americans of the Central Plains made travel in that area dangerous. Soldiers at the fort protected the settlers and were responsible for safe mail delivery.

The site has nine buildings with barracks and officer's quarters. Fort Larned has been restored to look as it did in the late 1800s.

KENTUCKY

Cumberland Gap National Historical Park

Cumberland Gap National Historical Park is in Middlesboro, Kentucky. The Gap forms the border of Kentucky, Tennessee, and Virginia. The Gap is a natural break in the Appalachian Mountain chain. It was used by animals and Native Americans long before it was discovered by the first white explorers. It is estimated that between 1775 and 1810, more than 200,000 people used the gap to cross into Kentucky.

LOUISIANA

French Quarter

The French Quarter in New Orleans is one of the most famous sites in Louisiana. The narrow streets of the French Quarter are lined with old houses that combine French and Spanish designs. The famous Saint Louis Cathedral faces Jackson Square in the heart of the French Quarter. Each year in February, the area hosts the largest Mardi Gras celebration in the U.S. Mardi Gras is a Roman Catholic festival.

MAINE

Acadia National Park

Acadia National Park is located along Maine's Atlantic Coast. The park includes some of the rocky islands off the coast. Native Americans lived in the area more than 5,000 years ago. A nature center and museum displays some of the relics found there. The rocky coastline and inland mountains are home to hundreds of species of birds and other wildlife. Porpoises, seals, and whales swim off the coast. The best views of the park are from Cadillac Mountain, the highest point in the area.

MARYLAND

Antietam National Battlefield Site

An important battle of the Civil War occurred along Antietam Creek in 1862. Led by General Robert E. Lee, nearly 50,000 Confederate troops invaded the North. Union General George McClellan's 70,000 troops met Lee's army at the creek. The horrible battle that followed left more than 4,000 soldiers dead. Thousands more were wounded. General Lee and his troops retreated across the Potomac River the next day, ending the battle. The area was named a National Battlefield Site in 1890.

MASSACHUSETTS
Plymouth Rock

    We have all learned about the Pilgrims and their dangerous voyage to the New World on the *Mayflower*. According to legend, they landed at Plymouth Rock. Plymouth Rock is in the town of Plymouth, Massachusetts. The Pilgrims named Plymouth after the city they departed from—Plymouth, England. Tourists of Plymouth can visit a museum, a full-scale model of the *Mayflower*, and Burial Hill Cemetery, where several of the Pilgrims are buried.

MICHIGAN

Keweenaw National Historical Park

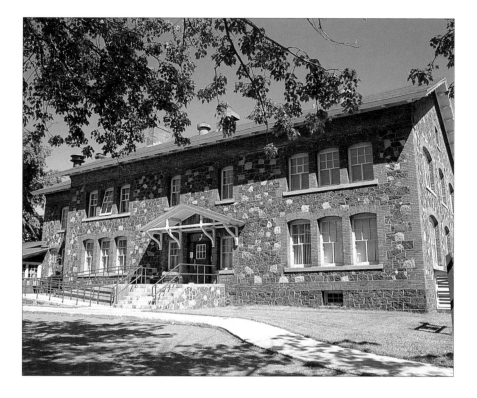

This historical park celebrates the area's long history of copper mining. The Keweenaw peninsula is the only place in the world where large amounts of natural copper can be found. Metal has been mined in this area for more than 7,000 years. Some of the more recent mines reach more than 9,000 feet (2,743 m) deep. That's close to 2 miles (3.2 km)! The National Park Service provides guided tours in the park.

MINNESOTA

Grand Portage National Monument

Grand Portage National Monument lies on the shore of Lake Superior in Grand Marais, Minnesota. The monument is in the Grand Portage Indian Reservation. The area was home to the Ojibwe Indians for hundreds of years. The Grand Portage connected Lake Superior to a series of lakes and rivers. Traders, explorers, and settlers used the portage to begin their journeys into the interior of North America. The area was also a trading center.

MISSISSIPPI

Brices Cross Roads National Battlefield

Brices Cross Roads National Battlefield honors the memory of those who struggled through the Civil War period. The Battle of Brices Cross Roads started June 10, 1864. Confederate forces led by General Nathan Bedford Forrest fought a larger Union force led by General Samuel Davis Sturgis. Somehow, General Forrest and his troops defeated the Union army. They captured 1,500 Union soldiers and their artillery.

MISSOURI

Jefferson National Expansion Memorial

The Jefferson National Expansion Memorial includes the Gateway Arch, the Museum of Westward Expansion, and St. Louis' Old Courthouse. The Arch stands 630 feet (192 m) tall and is made of stainless steel. It was designed by Eero Saarnen. Its design was chosen as a monument to the spirit of western pioneers. The museum is just below the Arch. It holds a collection of western artifacts including an American Indian tipi.

MONTANA

Little Bighorn Battlefield
National Monument

A famous battle took place here between the U.S. Army and a force of Native Americans. A large group of warriors from the Sioux, Cheyenne, Lakota, and Arapaho nations met a smaller group of cavalry led by Lieutenant Colonel George Custer. A fierce battle followed. Custer and his men were killed. The battle is known as "Custer's Last Stand." Visitors to the monument can walk the grounds where the battle took place.

NEBRASKA

The Homestead National Monument of America

This monument was set aside in 1936 to preserve one of the first Nebraska homesteads. Daniel and Agnes Freeman were among the first settlers to take land based on the Homestead Act. The Homestead Act stated that any citizen could claim up to 160 acres (64.75 ha) of government land. Homesteaders had to agree to build a home and grow crops on the land. Thousands of homesteaders soon followed. The park includes a visitors' center, an historic log cabin, and the Freeman School.

NEVADA

Hoover Dam

Hoover Dam is on the border of Nevada and Arizona. The dam was built between 1931 and 1936. It is named after President Herbert Hoover. The dam is huge. It stands 726 feet (221 m) high and is 1,244 feet (379 m) long. Lake Mead, created by the dam, is one of the largest man-made lakes in the world. Hoover Dam makes electricity for Arizona, California, and Nevada.

NEW HAMPSHIRE

Saint-Gaudens National Historic Site

Augustus Saint-Gaudens was an American sculptor. He lived from 1848-1907. His most famous work is a bronze statue of Abraham Lincoln. It stands in Lincoln Park in Chicago, Illinois. Another Saint-Gaudens statue is of General William Sherman on a horse. Sherman was a Civil War general. The statue is in New York City's Central Park. Saint-Gaudens' home and studio in New Hampshire are open for the public to tour.

NEW JERSEY

Edison National Historic Site

    The Thomas Edison Laboratory in West Orange, New Jersey, was the site of many great inventions. Thomas Edison worked there from 1887 until his death in 1931. Edison is known for inventing the light bulb and for his work with telegraph machines. Many of Edison's other inventions were created at his West Orange Laboratory. The motion picture camera and alkaline batteries are two inventions that came from the laboratory.

NEW MEXICO

Aztec Ruins National Monument

This monument was established in 1923. It is located in northwestern New Mexico. Within the monument are the ruins of a prehistoric Native American village, or pueblo. Although named for the Aztec people of Mexico, there is no known connection. The largest section of the ruin was built nearly 900 years ago. Made of masonry and timber, the pueblo stood three stories tall and contained 500 rooms.

New York

Statue of Liberty National Monument

The Statue of Liberty is one of the largest statues in the world. It is known around the world as a symbol of freedom. The statue was a gift from France to the United States. It celebrates the first 100 years of American independence. The statue stands on Liberty Island in New York Harbor. It became a National Monument in 1924.

North Carolina

Wright Brothers National Memorial

An historic event occurred at this site on December 17, 1903. The event was the world's first successful manned flight in a heavier-than-air craft. The airplane was built by brothers Orville and Wilbur Wright. They each made two flights that day. The longest, by Wilbur, went 852 feet (260 m) and lasted a whopping 59 seconds. Visitors to the site near Kitty Hawk, North Carolina, can explore a museum and tour the flight trail. A granite monument was erected at the site in 1932.

North Dakota

Theodore Roosevelt National Park

More than 70,000 acres (28,328 ha) of rugged landscape make up the Theodore Roosevelt National Park. Roosevelt loved this area of the United States. He once said, "I would not have been President had it not been for my experience in North Dakota." Bison, elk, deer, eagles, and prairie dogs make their homes in the park. The restored Roosevelt home on "Elkhorn Ranch" sits in the central section of the park.

OHIO

Perry's Victory and International Peace Memorial

Oliver Hazard Perry once said, "We have met the enemy and they are ours." He was talking about the Battle of Lake Erie in the War of 1812. Commodore Perry led a fleet of U.S. naval ships that attacked a British fleet near Put-In-Bay on Lake Erie. The U.S. fleet captured or destroyed the entire British fleet. The victory gave the U.S. control over Lake Erie. The Peace Memorial was built in 1912.

OKLAHOMA

Fort Sill Military Reservation
and National Historic Landmark

Soldiers began building Fort Sill in 1869. Soldiers were stationed there to stop Indian attacks on settlers. Frontier scouts such as "Buffalo Bill" Cody and "Wild Bill" Hickok joined the soldiers in their attacks on the hostile Indians. The Indians finally surrendered. The soldiers' new job was to protect the Indians from outlaws and thieves. Today the fort is an active military base. It houses the U.S. Army Field Artillery School.

OREGON

Oregon Trail

    Almost 2,000 miles (3,219 km) long, the Oregon Trail led from Independence, Missouri, to the Columbia River in Oregon. Thousands of pioneers traveled the route to reach the American Northwest. Travelers risked starvation, illness, extreme weather, and possible Indian attack. The journeys sometimes took 6 months. The stone marker seen here marks the end of the trail in Oregon.

PENNSYLVANIA

Gettysburg National Military Park

Gettysburg, Pennsylvania, was the site of the largest battle ever fought in the Western Hemisphere. More than 50,000 soldiers were killed, wounded, or captured there. The 3-day battle was considered to be a turning point in the Civil War. The Union Army turned back the Confederate invasion into the North. The National Military Park includes the Soldiers National Cemetery and nearly 6,000 acres (2,428 ha) of monuments, markers, and memorials.

RHODE ISLAND

Roger Williams National Memorial

    The Roger Williams National Memorial honors Roger Williams—the founder of Rhode Island. Williams was a member of a group of Puritan Christians in England. They were mistreated because of their religious beliefs. Many Puritans, including Williams, moved to America. Williams started Rhode Island colony in present-day Providence. Williams chose to build the colony by a natural spring. The memorial includes a park on 4.6 acres (1.9 ha) at the original spring location.

SOUTH CAROLINA

Fort Sumter National Monument

Fort Sumter is a historic fort in Charleston, South Carolina. It was the site of the first battle of the Civil War. On April 12, 1861, shots were fired marking the beginning of the Civil War. After a 34-hour battle, the Union army surrendered the fort to the Confederates. The Confederate army held the fort through 22 months of battles until the end of the war.

SOUTH DAKOTA

Mount Rushmore National Memorial

It took 14 years for Gutzon Borglum and 400 workers to sculpt Mount Rushmore. The sculpture is carved out of granite in the Black Hills. The busts of Presidents George Washington, Thomas Jefferson, Theodore Roosevelt, and Abraham Lincoln represent the first 150 years of American history. A new visitors' center, a museum, and walking trails welcome tourists to the memorial.

TENNESSEE

Great Smoky Mountains National Park

The Great Smoky Mountains National Park is one of the most popular parks in the United States. The park is named for the smoke-like haze that often covers the mountains. Hundreds of thousands of people visit the park each year. They enjoy the beautiful hiking trails and fishing streams. If a visitor is lucky, he or she may spot a famous local resident—a black bear.

TEXAS
The Alamo

When you visit the Alamo, it may seem strange to see it surrounded by hotels and department stores. The city of San Antonio has grown up around the Spanish Mission. The Alamo is known for a battle between Mexican soldiers and a group of determined Texans. About 4,000 Mexican soldiers attacked the Alamo in 1836. 187 Texans defended the Alamo. Davy Crockett and James Bowie were among them. After 11 days the Mexicans finally broke through and killed all of the Texans.

Utah

Arches National Park

    In 1971 Arches National Monument became a national park. Hundreds of natural arches can be seen in the 73,000-acre (29,542-ha) park. The arches, made of reddish sandstone, were formed over hundreds of thousands of years. Wind, rain, and extreme temperatures eroded the rock into beautiful shapes. The largest arch is Landscape Arch. It is 100 feet (30 m) tall and 291 feet (89 m) wide.

VERMONT

Battle of Bennington

The Battle of Bennington was fought during the American Revolution. On August 16, 1777, a force of British soldiers and Native Americans attacked an American supply base near Bennington, Vermont. A militia from Vermont and New Hampshire defended the base and easily won. Two hundred and seven British and Indians were killed or wounded. More than 600 were taken prisoner. The American militia lost only 14 men.

VIRGINIA

Mount Vernon

President George Washington and his wife Martha made Mount Vernon their home in 1759. The three-story wood home sits on a hill. At one time it was surrounded by 8,000 acres (3,238 ha) of land. Although Washington loved his home, he spent little time there. His political life kept him busy.

The President and his wife are buried close to the house. The Mount Vernon Ladies Association has maintained Mount Vernon since 1860.

WASHINGTON
Mount St. Helens
National Volcano Monument

For more than 100 years Mount St. Helens was quiet. And then suddenly, in 1980, the volcano began to show signs of life. That May, the volcano exploded with terrific force. The entire mountaintop was blown off. The eruption threw a cloud of ash and debris 12 miles (19 km) into the air. Sixty people died. All plant and animal life within 70 square miles (180 sq km) was destroyed. Mount St. Helens became a national monument in 1982.

WEST VIRGINIA

Harpers Ferry National Historical Park

Harpers Ferry was the site of a U.S. arsenal and armory in the late 1790s. Many rifles used in the Civil War were made there. It was also the site of several Civil War battles. A famous raid by abolitionist (a person who wants to stop slavery) John Brown occurred there in 1859. Brown and his men took control of the armory.

The monument was established in 1944. In 1963 it became a National Historical Park. The monument includes several old buildings that have been turned into museums.

WISCONSIN

Apostle Islands National Lakeshore

Apostle Islands National Lakeshore consists of 21 islands and 12 miles (19.3 km) of beach on Wisconsin's Lake Superior shoreline. Visitors can explore old-growth forests and beautiful sea caves. Historic sites in the area include stone quarries, old logging camps, and historic lighthouses. Many people also enjoy fishing, canoeing, kayaking, and watching wildlife.

WYOMING

Devils Tower National Monument

Devils Tower became the nation's first national monument in 1906. The tower, located in northeastern Wyoming, is 865 feet (264 m) high. It was probably formed by an ancient volcano. Sioux Indians called the tower "Mateo Tepee," which means Grizzly Bear's Lodge. A Sioux legend tells the story of a giant bear that left deep scratch marks on the sides of the tower. The bear was trying to climb the tower to reach some Indians that were on top.